"AUDITION POEMS"

"AUDITION POEMS"

Inspiration on the fly
Published by PoemCatcher Creations
Salisbury Centre
2 Salisbury Road
Edinburgh, EH16 5AB

Copyright
All the poems in this book were donated with love and permission to be published. It would be thievery to steal the copyright from the authors. It remains their own. This is their beautiful creativity and I am just a creative collator. Use of this material is welcomed – providing it inspires, engages and enthrals audiences

Each and every poem in this book is brilliant. If you disagree, send £10 with your complaint to a child in Haiti.

Cover Design by Trevor at Fresh Digital
ISBN978-0-9567645-0-8

This book was made in 6 hours at Britain's' Got Talent First round auditions in Glasgow, Dec 2010.

Visit www.poemcatcher.com for other titles including
"QUAKE – Built from nothing"
"BALLS from the queue" Wimbledon tennis poems
"FUNGUS POEMS"
"SALTY poems from the Sea"
"FANTASTIC FIREWORKS"
"HAUNTED HALLOWEEN"

About PoemCatcher Creations

The Pavement PoemCatcher wanders the streets of festivals and events begging for fresh poems to be written "on the fly". Nearly every poem that is donated gets published, creating books with poetic snapshots that capture the public experience and delight the reader.

He has done this since sitting down on a pavement in march 2010 to beg for poems for the people of Haiti.

By spontaneously asking "DONATE A POEMS" he inspires brilliance, encourages 'raw' creativity, and fundraises for charity

www.poemcatcher.com
inspiration@poemcatcher.com

Charity Donation

£2 from the sale of this book are donated to MOVEMBER fundraising initiatives – supporting The Prostate Cancer Charity

"Growing positive masculinity – right under your nose"

References

*I am so full of admiration for the way you captured people to donate their poems, especially those that thought they couldn't write. This a great testament to your personality'
What you have is: 'A wonderful collection of poetry which mirrors the inner thoughts of a vast cross section of society'.*

Provost Stephanie Young of East Ayrshire Council
"QUAKE – Built from nothing"

"The engagement he was able to make with both participants and general public was truly remarkable, and this lead to some stunning contributions from all ages, genders and classes. People who wouldn't, or couldn't, have seen themselves as having an ounce of creativity were discovering new aspects of themselves - and enjoying it!"

Johns Shaw, Director, Fringe by the Seas 2010
"SALTY – Poems from the Sea"

"What Andrew does is magical. He has an uncanny ability to conjure and inspire even the most unlikely poet to create amazing poetry. My teenage kids think that the PoemCatcher is a 'Legend'."

Thomas Munro, Father & Husband, Scotland.
"Private Wedding Book"

About the messy bits...

Think, feel, doodle, make a list, ~~scratch some lines out~~, start again, find more paper, talk to your friends, gather ideas, just look around. They are here to be found.

Many of you did,
believed that you could
You did brilliant
I knew that you would
I love your first efforts
With edits and all
The edge of creation
A little bit raw.

P.S. this book is full of mistakes. Such is life.
Some are mine, some are yours.
I don't mind.
The struggle for perfectionism ain't worth the stress.
I far prefer a creative mess.

Table of Contents

About PoemCatcher Creations 3

Charity Donation 4

References 5

About the messy bits... 6

Table of Contents 7

BGT GLASGOW AUDITIONS... 11

    Hendo.. 12

    Judges.. 13

    Bears 14

    MWi@Dillychip 15

    BGT... 16

    Untitled 17

    Curse 18

    Riding in the Queue 19

    The Day 20

    Easy Does it 21

    Untitled 22

    Hours for Ours.. 23

    Ferrero Rocher... 24

    Chirsty BGT Experience 25

Stars	26
Untitled	27
Patience	28
The wonder of Celtic Thunder	29
Roadie	30
BGT	31
Ruin all we know	32
My Sing Bling Dream	33
Leonards young team	34
Elite	35
You have 3 Yes's!	36
Alone	37
Flying high	38
Anticipation	39
Pillar to Post	40
The Talent in Waiting	41
In the Que	42
Her nickname was MAZ	43
Why are we waiting?	44
WINTER	45
Talent!	46
Scared	47

- That's a bit much! ... 48
- Snow ... 49
- Rythm ... 50
- Letters to the Judges ... 51
  - My Letter ... 52
  - Jodi Has Talent! ... 53
  - J.P. Costello Letter ... 54
  - Bobbi's Letter ... 55
- Nearly Anonymous ... 56
  - Untitled ... 57
  - Waiting! Waiting! ... 58
  - Auditions ... 59
  - Sare Feet ... 60
  - Warriors ... 61
  - Hansum ... 62
  - The man in the tartan skirt ... 63
  - BGT ... 64
  - Q ... 65
  - Birthday ... 66
  - Simon Cowell Says ... 67
  - Sing the Talk ... 68
  - Paige Kerr ... 69

Polish Poem	70
Briatan are the Best	71
BGT is rubbish	72
Mum and Talent	73
Pushy Mums	74
Untitled	75
Untitled	76
Write a fresh poem here	77
Index of Authors	78
From the PoemCatcher	80
Apologies (from you to me)	81
From other PoemCatcher Books	82
Atlas	84
Ode to SW19	86
Trailer Ode	87
Directed Panspermia	89
Treasure Hunt	90
A Nameless Villanelle	92
We stayed in a Flat	93
"............"	95
October Thiefs	98
Jack O' Lantern	99

BGT GLASGOW AUDITIONS

Hendo

There was a young girl from Troon
Who everyone knew was a loon
She was nervous about her audition
Which was a Natasha Beddingfield rendition
But boy that girl could croon!

By Jules
71795

Judges

Simon Cowel is going to scowl

Piers Morgen is gonna sing all morning

Amanda Holden takes all the oldn's

By Matthew Gow
72068

Bears

Little baby Salmon
Swimming up the stream
to find some carbonara
cooked with extra cream.

Jimmy Buffett loves it
to see a salmon swim
so when i grow up big and strong
I want to be like him.

Also ...BEARS!

By Craig Seton and Brady (+bears)

MWi@Dillychip

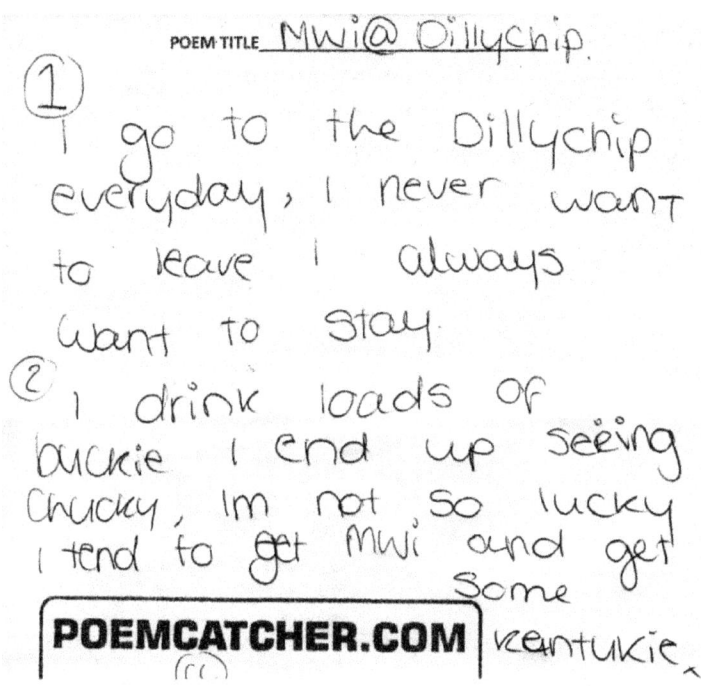

By Fern, April & Isabel

BGT

At BGT we wait in a Queue
The PoemCatcherman is passing through
the sights to see when waiting to go on
can show the world can work as one

By Valgill

Untitled

We have had to wait
So long.
So my cousin can sing
One song.

By Charlotte Tasker

Curse

Shakes, Cracks
Shifted Shape.
The Pearl upon The Obsidian
Blankie calls it out!
No more me,
But a lost soul
I cry. It hates this fleshy cage!
Outside the wolves begin to howl!

By Brandon Campbell
71866

Riding in the Queue

Here I am
Standing in a queue
wondering is I am good enough
to sing a song for you.

By Megan McWaters
71986

The Day

Today is a great day
We thought we'd audition, what, the hey
The queue goes on and on and on...
it's far to long!
I don't want to wait no more
So please let me go through the door!

By Lauren Smith
72014

Easy Does it

POEM TITLE: easy does it

Sick with the Rythm
sick with the flow
Click to the scene quick.
I AM Strict to Explode,
I bust a ryhme then
I flip to a mode
The line gets bigger
but I'll Rip tha Show!

By CERI-P
71668

Untitled

HE SAYS HE ISNT NERVOUS
HE'S EXCITED TO BE HERE
DAD AND I ARE SO PROUD
C'MON LUKE WE LOUDLY
                    CHEER.

By Lynda McLauchlan
72072

Hours for Ours

POEM TITLE: Hours For Ours

We've practiced for hours
We've waited for hours
We hope 3 "Yes's" are ours

By Kirsty Hill & Connie McCrone
71902

Ferrero Rocher...

James Boyd's appeared on BGT on two previous occasions- attempting to set Guinness world records for eating the most Ferrero Rocher & After Eight Chocolates in a minute.
Here is his poem

DONATE A POEM
Please donate a brilliant, fresh, creative poem.
Themes to inspire you are "YES!", "JUDGES" & "TALENT"

POEM TITLE: Ferrero Rockers & After 8

I went on BGT to attempt
Ferrero Rockers and I failed,
I ate After 8 Mints and I
again failed.
I hope again not to
fail but I said
up to semi-finals.

James Graham Boyd
BGT 2009 & 2010

By James Boyd

Chirsty BGT Experience

Britain's Got Talent I am here to sing,
But standing in this Q is not my thing,
I hope and pray my time will come soon,
To go up on the stage and give them a tune.
All my friends will be proud of me
If I get onto the T.V.
So C'mon judges give me a chance,
I'll even do a little dance.

By ChirstyHarkins
71897

Stars

Stars in the sky,
So bright
I look at them and
Think of you
All of you who
looked at them
Once just like me.
One day somebody
will remember me just
like I remember the ones
before me...

By Tunafriel

Untitled

POEM TITLE: UNTITLED

AND IF MY HEART SHOULD WEEP
THESE TEARS WOULD FALL UPON MY SOUL
BUT NEVER DAMPEN DREAMS OF LOVE
THAT BRING FORTH GREAT JOY
AND EVERLASTING PASSION.

By Paul Dempster

Patience

There's a queue in the SECC
There's Sammy, Tom, Dick, Harry and me
All crossin' our legs
Everyone of us begs
For God's sake let us out for a pee.

By Ronnie Cullins
71869

The wonder of Celtic Thunder

The crowd did wonder
when Celtic Thunder
came onto the stage.

Simon did laugh
Amanda Squeaked
And Piers was in a rage.

All around, were gripped by sound
Of Taiko at its best
Strange cultures from around the world
Including East & West.

And when the act did stop
The audience was in awe
Simon just turned to Piers
and said "Jings, that was awfy braw"

By Glen Alexander
71549

Roadie

Hey Jodie,
I'm the Roadie,
I carry equipment.
I am made of cement,
I don't have a beard
But I am a bit weird
And I'll never be on
Britains Got Talent

By Scummings
666

BGT

POEM TITLE: BGT

BGT, BGT
we're going to be on TV!
BGT, BGT
WE better not hear a BEEP, BEEP, BEEP

Simon, Simon, he's the man
Amanda holden, she's so calm
pers, pers, he's a moan
all he does is groan, groan, groan!
and by the way glasgow has talent

POEMCATCHER.COM

By Mekala & Emma

Ruin all we know

Is there really such a thing as peace?
Or is that confused with tranquillity & serenity
Whatever way you put it I love the quietness
For me to keep in mind what's best for me and I
choose to take my love and go slow
there's no need to rush life, and I don't need to live by these
lives that we're told, that are sold in magazines
so I take it easy, then my life is a breeze.

By Chaz B

My Sing Bling Dream

POEM TITLE: My sing bling dream!!

Go Go what a brilliant show
I'm here to sing but I can't
dae it without my bling
bling! Yo Yo wheres mah rng!?
when you hear me sing
Your head will spin and
I will be waiting for the phone
to ring.... got ~~that~~ simon?
we know your all a brilliant
team but don't forget the
name NASREEN!! ♡

POEMCATCHER.COM

By Nasreen
72076

Leonards young team

A don't know why a should be helping you
cause think about it, We've contestants too
Your walking about with some stupid pole
You've probably never had your hole
What the hell you meant to be
You'll probably never get on T.V.
Lets face it you're not gonna win
So go stick yer trashy poems in the bin
So we're wishing you good luck
If you don't like our poem
Get tae ****

By Little Contestants

Elite

POEM TITLE: Elite

Elites Poem!!

We are a dance group from Brownie!,
in Edinburgh we bide,
Wi Pom Poms, batons + Maces,
We take it all in our stride.
At Britains got Talent,
We come as a fleet,
We are the dance troupe
thats called ELITE!!

By ELITE

You have 3 Yes's!

POEM TITLE: You have 3 Yesses!

"You have 3 Yesses"
I didn't beleive them, they were lying and then it hit me. My pulse raced and I could feel the thudding in my chest. I did it, it was over. The undescribable desire to scream with joy tookover and I knew I'd completley embarassed myself on National T.V. but I didn't care. I did it. I made it.

By Kailiegh Thompson
72018

Alone

I'm sitting here
All Alone
Looking out at
All the faces
The room is packed
But I'm all alone
As the feat eats
Up inside me.
So I have a chance
Is it my time
to live the dream
inside me.

By Lauren Logue
78045

Flying high

Flying, flying, high in the sky
the talent is yours so don't hide
Born, Born the talent is yours so
show us you are a dreamer
The dream is yours
and you can achieve.

By Telma Brown
71131

Anticipation

POEM TITLE ~~The~~ Anticipation

I cannae believe,
I'm in the que.
for britains got talent.
In the hope to Impress you.
I'm nervos, I'm Scared
I'm excited too
but it will all be worth it,
If I get through!

By Simone Kelly
71811

Pillar to Post

First in a queue to go to a table
into another queue to pick up a lable
then to a queue for area C
with everyone else, the band and me.

For a chance to perform on a big TV stage
We queued and we queued for what seemed like an age
For nearly 5 hours passed from host to host
we were shunted all over from pillar to post

By Stewart

The Talent in Waiting

BGT is the best
and if you hate it you're a pest
dancing singing lots to do
there's always a talent for you.

~~~~

Moving, shaking, dancers galore
Gymnasts stretch & bend , splits on the floor
Drag queens, drummers, Girls with Pom-Poms
Michael Jackson on his lonesome
People laughing, smiling, anticipation
Through to the next round
The fun in waiting.

By Stephanie Eva McGuire Reid
71511

In the Que

Standing here for hours
waiting to play to impress
the judges on a special day
Hope I get on T.V
Someday.

By Billy McGinnis
71771

Her nickname was MAZ

I woke up to the sound of a love,
surely it had to be love,
I looked up to the stars above...
The stars read her sweet name,
The first I Sell for that dame
I live and die for her I'd claim
but when she slipped away,
I was to blame.

By Matthew Quinn

Why are we waiting?

Been here for several hours
feels like all night and day
asking people for poems
In every single way.

I feel I'm something different
a new talent, yes I am
I'll take Subo by storm
be the next best talent woman.

By Lynsey Braidwood

WINTER

Winter is coming and the snow is too

Ice covers the ground to play with you

Nice and warm in your cosy house

Tucked up snugly like a mouse

Everybody enjoys a winter day

Robin red breast fly away

By Lauren Curtis
71813

Talent!

The Judges, the lights, the wondering

Along the way you get a yes or a no.

Late at night you are still wondering and waiting

Excited wether or not you are going to get through.

Next time I'll bring a picnic

Talent is not a great

By Nieve McQuillan
71805

Scared

POEM TITLE: Scared

he's just gone in
So scared for him,
I hope he sings well,
and puts the judges under
his spell

By Hannah McLaughlan
72072

That's a bit much!

POEM TITLE: That's a bit Much!

Ahh BRILIANT!!
The crack in Orkney!
Ahh BRILIANT!!
Whats in the cupboard??
Ahh BRILIANT!!

By Shane Donnelly
71773

Snow

Snow is bold
Snow is cold
Snow kills old people
When they are old
Snow is white
Snow is bright
It falls down in the middle
of the night
in Glasgae

By Lolybabe
71835

Rythm

Treble jump in, treble, treble jump in
and treble and treble and treble and toe
See the Irish dancers' feet flow
Treble jump in, treble, treble jump in
Britain's Got Talent

    We are going to win.

By Siamsoir Irish Dancers
70010

Letters to the Judges

My Letter

DONATE A POEM
Please donate a brilliant, fresh, creative poem.
Themes to inspire you are "YES!", "JUDGES" & "TALENT"

POEM TITLE: My LEtter

Dear ~~Amanda~~ Amanda

I'm very happy to be here thanks for Britains got talent i'm looking forward to do my audition I hope I get through, I'll do all I can to impress you and the judges thanks for picking myself for this oppertunity

Love -
Ashley

POEMCATCHER.COM
This fabulous poem is donated with love and may happily be published
Poet's Name: Ashley Brown
Email: ???@??.?

Audition Number: 71802

By Ashley Brown
71802

Jodi Has Talent!

Jodi is a star
She has travelled from afar
we think she has a chance
of winning with her dance.

Simon, Amanda and Peirs
Will really think she's fierce
she always tries her best
So Go on, all three say YES!

By Karen Maclean
71650

J.P. Costello Letter

POEM TITLE J P Costello

Dear Suman you should have received my CD and letter b now you have nd replied Hope you liked it
Sincerely
JP Costello

POEMCATCHER.COM

By J.P. Costello

Bobbi's Letter

Dear Simon,

Today has been a very long day but well worth it. I'm looking forward to addition but I'm very nervous. I met a nice girl today thanks to Britens got talent. I really hope I've done enough I'm hoping I get through and if I get through and get to the stage in this show I'll get to meed you and the other judges I hope you enjoy everything I do. I've tried very hard.

POEMCATCHER.COM

This fabulous poem is donated with love and may happily be published

Poet's Name: Bobbi Evermayor

Email: ▅▅▅▅▅▅▅▅▅▅▅▅

Audition Number: 71848

By Bobbi
71848

Nearly Anonymous

Untitled

Writing a poem for the PoemCatcher
I can't write it just now
So I will write it after...

Hear am back again
Hope to go for my
audition in ten
really excited
It I get through...
I will be delighted.

By Carla

Waiting! Waiting!

Mackem/Geordie (via Yorkshire) Collaboration

Once i saw a little worm
a crawling on its belly
I watched it for a little
Then squashed it with me wellie

OR

Then served it in my deli

By Shelia Shiela
71637

Auditions

So many people young and old
Happily waiting in a room to hold
on to the chance to sing or play
and make Britain's Got Talents'
Judges Day!

By 71435

Sare Feet

Oh, Ma feet are aching
Stawning aw this time
But its well worth the wait
For ma wee son O' mine.

Warriors

Standing in line for BGT
All of us have wobbly knees
Scary faces and scary hair
We are the warriors

BEWARE!

By Olivia and Brooklyn
71777 & 71780

Hansum

How about a turkey
for breakfast or tea?

How about a hansum man
for you and for me.

This is a poem about
turkey and hansum men.

P.S. not you!

The man in the tartan skirt

Once there was a man in a
tarted skirt he went round
People asking them to write a
Poem to fill his net, but
People wondered why he
Wants this, these are the
questions that haunt me.

BGT

We're in the queue for BGT
The holding room is massive
Although the competitions fierce
The people are really passive!!

By Eddie
71463

Q

      Singers, dancers
      Lots of chancers
      Here we stand in this queue
      Haven't got a damn clue
      What lies ahead
      But we stand instead
      Dreams in our head.

By Stina
72015

Birthday

Today is my birthday.
What am I to do?
I know sing, what else
That's what I will do.

Well nothing else is planned
Anne Francis

By Anne Francis

Simon Cowell Says

There's a hunky guy on my TV set
I'd really like to date
They say I'll never do it
Do you wanna bet?
Together we'd be great

I've got beautiful hair
Simon Cowell says
Better looking than some
Simon Cowell says
I've got fabulous legs
Simon Cowell says
And a fantastic...smile!!!

By Barbie Buckfast
71459

Sing the Talk

Waiting here in a big dark hall
Havin a laugh at them havin a ball
Hope they can sing as good as they talk
Cos they won't like it when the judges mock.

By Andy Truten

Paige Kerr

When you're standing in this long que
and you're starting to get scared
Just get to the end of the que
stand on the stage and picture
Them all in their underwear.

Then you hop up on that stage
and you're ready to sing your song
But scared in case you mess it up
Or get the words wrong

So just do your act
and do it good
and hopefully you'll get through
like you hoped you would.

Polish Poem

I understand that this is a "famous" or at least "well-known" polish poem. It was genuinely written in the queue, and references the original author.

POEM TITLE: Pan Tadeusz
Adam Mickiewicz

Litwo, Ojczyzno moje
Ty jesteś jak zdrowie,
ile Cię trzeba cenić ten tylko
się dowie,
kto Cię utracił.
Dziś piękność Twą w całej ozdobie
Widzę i opisuję, bo tęsknię po Tobie.

Briatan are the Best

DONATE A POEM
Please donate a brilliant, fresh, creative poem.
Themes to inspire you are "YES!", "JUDGES" & "TALENT"

POEM TITLE: BRIATAN ARE The BEST

BRitian are the best the best, the best, the best. Scotland are the best the best. ENgland are the best the best the best at one thing Britian got talent.

POEMCATCHER.COM

This fabulous poem is donated with love and may happily be published

Poet's Name: Guy Shafar age 9

Email: ███████████

Audition Number: 7672

By Guy Shafar

BGT is rubbish

I hate waiting its really
Boring.
and now I'm stuck writing a
Poem
When will this nightmare ever
End
Britain's Got Talent is driving me
Round the Bend!

By an Unhappy Citizen

Mum and Talent

My Mum is on Britans got talent. My Mum is going to try to win it. the end.

By Holly McGee
71791

Pushy Mums

Ours daughters say we're pushy
But we don't agree
We've only made them sing and dance
Since the age of three

We dragged them to auditions
And they said what the heck
But we're going to make them do it
So we'd meet Ant and Dec.

By Karen and Lauren
(Pushy Mums Extraordinaire!)

Untitled

Sitting, waiting to find out if we become stars
Sometimes its boring
Sometimes its exciting
But for everyone here, Its an exciting event
in our lives

Untitled

> The spring has sprung
> The grass has Riz
> I wonder where the
> Birdie's is

By Connor Seaton
72029

Write a fresh poem here

Hopefully you're feeling inspired – so here's a page for you to write another poem...or a letter to Simon

Index of Authors

70010, 51
71131, 39
71435, 60
71459, 68
71463, 65
71511, 42
71549, 30
71637, 59
71650, 54
71668, 22
71771, 43
71773, 49
71777, 62
71780, 62
71795, 13
71802, 53
71805, 47
71811, 40
71813, 46
71848, 56
71866, 19
71869, 29
71897, 26
71902, 24
71986, 20
72014, 21
72015, 66
72018, 37
72029, 77
72068, 14
72072, 23, 48

72076, 34
78045, 38
Andy Truten, 69
Anne Francis, 67
Ashley Brown, 53
Barbie Buckfast, 68
Billy McGinnis, 43
Bobbi, 56
Brady, 15
Brandon Campbell, 19
Carla, 58
CERI-P, 22
Charlotte Tasker, 18
Chaz B, 33
ChirstyHarkins, 26
Connie McCrone, 24
Connor Seaton, 77
Craig Seton, 15
Eddie, 65
ELITE, 36
Fern, April & Isabel, 16
Glen Alexander, 30
Guy Shafar, 72
Hannah McLaughlan, 48
Holly McGee, 74
J.P. Costello, 55
James Boyd, 25
Jules, 13
Kailiegh Thompson, 37
Karen and Lauren, 75
Karen Maclean, 54

Kirsty Hill, 24
Lauren Curtis, 46
Lauren Logue, 38
Lauren Smith, 21
Little Contestant, 35
Lolybabe, 50
Lynda McLauchlan, 23
Lynsey Braidwood, 45
Matthew Gow, 14
Matthew Quinn, 44
Megan McWaters, 20
Mekala & Emma, 32
Nasreen, 34
Nieve McQuillan, 47
Olivia and Brooklyn, 62

Paul Dempster, 28
Ronnie Cullins, 29
Scummings, 31
Shane Donnelly, 49
Shelia Shiela, 59
Siamsoir Irish Dancers, 51
Simone Kelly, 40
Stephanie Eva McGuire Reid, 42
Stewart, 41
Stina, 66
Telma Brown, 39
Tunafriel, 27
Unhappy Citizen, 73
Valgill, 17

From the PoemCatcher

Apologies (from you to me)

Dear PoemCatcher

Sorry for the handwriting that you could not read, and sorry for the metric rhythm that you could not follow and sorry for not giving the poem a title, and thank you, so much for giving it a title for me (why didn't you just ask?, I would have done it happily) and I forgive you for typing up the most poignant moment of the poem with the wrong word. (I promise to write neater next time).

Oh, don't worry about the auto-capitalising of all the little-letters I so carefully choose to punctuate. I understand the nuances of word-processing in a hurry.

Lastly sorry for not seeing my own brilliance. I wrote a great poem and then dissed it myself. I've had time to reflect and I'm pretty chuffed that I could write such an amazing poem so spontaneously. I really like my own poem. I was brilliant.

I promise to write some more

With Love
The Aspirational Poet

From other PoemCatcher Books

Enjoy a few favourite poems from these other titles

www.poemcatcher.com
inspiration@poemcatcher.com

QUAKE Built from Nothing
Made in 4 days, begging for poems on the pavements of St Andrew's, as an unofficial one-man fringe event for StAnza poetry festival 2010

Atlas

    Brute Poseidon's insatiable wrath
    Spares no ship from tempest's path
    Argosie nor Spanish galleon
    Can halt the ocean's black battalion
        Nor shall mortal tools or toils
        Save our land-borne empires girth
        Should Altas shrug, he'll strew the oils,
    And stormy Quake shall drown the earth.

By Gavin Willow

QUAKE

Quake a dreadful wave beneath the ground
A wave of ruin, a crashing sound
A simple word with dreadful connotations
A terrible event that can and will destroy nations
Quake a dreadful wave beneath the ground
A wave of ruin, a final sound.

By Evan Dickson

BALLS from the Queue (Game, Set and Match)
A trilogy of tennis poems captured at Wimbledon 2010 in the infamous queue for centre court tickets.

Ode to SW19

> We're all sitting here on the grass
> Having a bit of a laugh
> At the lady in full union-Jack
> And outrageous red, white and blue hat
> Looking forward to drinking some Pimms
> On the hill that will always be Tim's
> We're hoping that Murray goes through
> But he's got so much more work left to do
> But while there's fresh air and sun
> We'll all have a ball and some fun
> Cos there's nothing to match
> A game, set and match
> So three cheers for
> Brill <u>Wimbledon!</u>

By Emma, Ruth and John.

Trailer Ode

To Wimbledon we do come to sell,

It's our idea of a working hell.

Burgers, sausages and bacon too,

We cook them all to the endless queue

They queue and camp in organized rows

With sun umbrellas and skimpy clothes

All in hope, but some in doubt

Of whether they can watch

From Murray Mount

By Terri McDonough

FUNGUS Poems
Mushroom and fungal poetry written by the world's leading scientists at the 9th international Mycology Conference in Edinburgh

Directed Panspermia

I have heard the humble mushroom spore
can travel to earth via meteor
able to survive both fire and frost
boundaries of space and time are crossed

Leading McKenna to hypothesize
on reasons why we are so wise
the curiosity of some ancient monkey
who stooped to nibble a cosmic fungi

An interaction with mushroom kind
which stretched his noggin, blew his mind
higher intelligence had landed.
human consciousness expanded.

By Kate Masters.

REFLECTIONS

Treasure Hunt

In a dark wood
Where no eyes can see
You could think that nothing's there
But no, don't just leave

Turn around a piece of bark
That lies on the withered leaves
Dig a bit with your Swiss knife
To expose the underneath
There, amongst the bugs and roots
A truffle waits for you and fruits.

By Heidi Tamm

SALTY Poems from the Sea

Capturing the delights of a British Summer festival in the Seaside town of North Berwick – during "Fringe By The Sea 2010" (This book includes a self-guided historic walking tour)

A Nameless Villanelle

Do not go gentle into city bright
Like moths attracted to unfettered flame
When summer days give way to autumn night.

Turn not your back on Law's unchallenged height
Or Bass Rock's craggy home to *Sula* fame
Do not go gentle into city bright.

Fair Scottish divas sang to gentle light
Till sleep and purest pleasure overcame
When summer days give way to autumn night.

Where waves lap languid on the shingle white
Where culture, coastal fringe to North Sea came
Do not go gentle into city bright.

Pause only, challenged soul, some verse to write
Let not the poem catcher miss his aim
When summer days give way to autumn night.

Do not in urban edifice excite
Nor bury self in fickle fancy's game
Do not go gentle into city bright
When summer days give way to autumn night.
By Lyle Crawford

We stayed in a Flat...

Called by the sea

near a Place named Melbourne, down under

the Burgh and the Seabird bluff

where the Firth furls forth and the Firth

faces north to its south-facing shore

in a Berwick north of Berwick

by an islet that May and a rock

of Bass in a shoal of isles

where the Links are linked

by Quality Street

and the hill is Law.

By Will Daunt

FANTASTIC FIREWORKS
Sparkling, explosive poetry from the Edinburgh festival Fireworks display.

"................."

Fireworks,
He wanted
Fireworks.

And they came,
Explosive
Magnificent!
Illumination!

Gone
In a flash
What was left?
Silence

Just silence

By Gillian Allen

The Coffee Shop Blues

Hitchcock & Bernstein's soaring scores
Scorch the air as the city roars
Crowds of tourists packed tae the hilt
Salute each other in fleece & kilt
Rebus, Rankine, murkrous crooks
Edinburgh & Scott, Ivanhoe & books
As diamond fireworks sparkle the sky,
I wipe a tear from my windstung eye
As another festival draws to a close
Auld Reekie inspires both poem and prose

By Kerry Black

HAUNTED HALLOWEEN

A creepy collection of haunted poems gathered in Auld Reekie (Edinburgh) over the festival weekend of Halloween and the pagan Samhuinn parade. (Celtic New Year) With poems written by ghouls and ghosts – you'll find this anthology slightly devilish, a tad mythical and honoring of the infamous Jack 'O Lantern.

October Thiefs

There's tapping at the window
There's footsteps on the floor
Howling in the darkness
Creaking in the door

Witches, bats and broomsticks
Fill the night time sky
Children scared to look up
On their night to sly

Illuminated pumpkins
with sharpened pumpkin teeth
shine from neighbours windows
to scare off little theifs

A song, a dance, a joke or two
to earn themselves a pound
As guisers fleece the neighbourhood
When halloween's around

By Keith Walker

Jack O' Lantern

Lights,

Peering out

I wonder

What he sees?

By Pam

www.ingramcontent.com/pod-product-compliance
Lightning Source LLC
Chambersburg PA
CBHW072100290426
44110CB00014B/1762